The excitement of the 1998 season has brought baseball back to the American forefront. With Mark McGwire and Sammy Sosa's summer-long chase for the home run record, the attention of millions has been captured. It has been an exciting, emotional, and heart-warming season as well, with both men displaying class and dignity, and in doing so shedding light on what is perhaps the greatest record in sports.

Roger Maris cherished the single-season home run record. It was something he was truly proud of. He would have been equally proud of the two men chasing his record, the feats they've accomplished, and the manner in which they have gone about it.

As true sportsmen, both Mark and Sammy are gentlemen on and off the field and represent dignity for the game. I am extremely happy for them and I know Roger would have felt the same way.

This was a season the Maris family will always remember.

Mrs. Roger Maris

Mrs. Roger Maris

The Great *Home Run Chase* of 1998

RACE FOR

Lee R. Schreiber

A **HarperEntertainment** Book
from HarperPerennial

Produced in Partnership with and licensed by
Major League Baseball Properties, Inc.

All acknowledgments can be found on page 119

FIRST EDITION

Designed by Jeannette Jacobs

ISBN 0–06–107359–8

98 99 00 01 02 ❖/RRD 10 9 8 7 6 5 4 3 2 1

C O N T E N T S

KEEPING PACE

Baseball keeps its own pace, moving in its own sweet time.

On a diamond-shaped chronometer, the pitcher's windup puts all hands in motion: hitters run counterclockwise; innings tick off **in steady, deliberate increments or, occasionally, race along with breathtaking swiftness.**

Seasons sweep and turn with their own rhythms and arcs, punctuating innings with moments so singular that for an instant a beat skips and the pace skids to a stop.

In this unforgettable baseball season, like no other in memory, singular moments skipped, stopped, ticked and raced in timely, rhythmic **bunches and timeless, sweeping arcs.**

On March 31, Opening Day in St. Louis, Cardinals first baseman Mark "Big Mac" McGwire—the defending home run champ with 58 dingers

accumulated in both leagues—hit his first four-bagger of the season, a grand slam. Pundits half-jokingly said he was on pace to clock 162 roundtrippers.

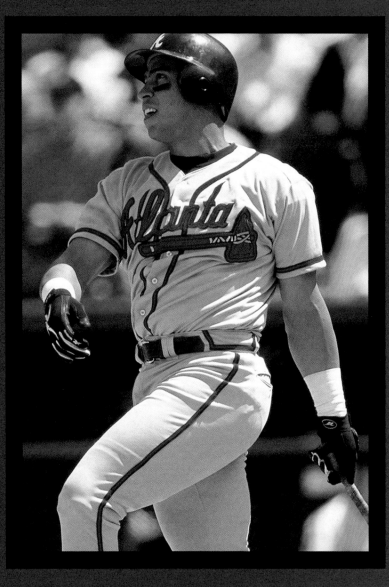

Within the first week McGwire went yard four times (which, if continued at that rate, would tally 130 home runs by year's end). **The pace was set. The race was on.** The first couple of months, several sluggers—Ken Griffey, Jr., Alex Rodriguez, Vinny Castilla, Greg Vaughn, Juan Gonzalez **and Andres "Big Cat" Galarraga—kept nipping at Big Mac's heels, but none could quite overtake him.**

As summer overtook spring,

Sammy Sosa's blistering 30-day pace propelled him past the pack, while Vinny and Juan just as suddenly dropped off the pace.

The dog days up and bit Big Cat and A-Rod, and soon slowed Vaughn and even Junior, leaving only the two big guns—Mac and Sammy—in the hunt.

JULY 28	MAC – 45	SAMMY – 41
AUG 8	MAC – 46	SAMMY – 44
AUG 11	MAC – 47	SAMMY – 46

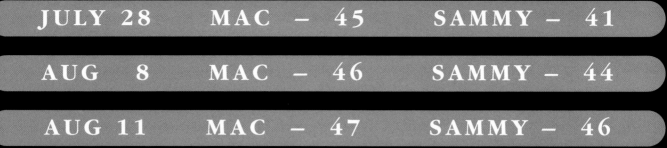

With two months to go, the pace really picked up. 🌑 *Back and over, up and out, going and gone . . . Every time Sosa threatened or tied for the lead, McGwire would respond in kind.* 🌑 *In the highly hyped Cardinals-Cubs matchup on August 19 in Chicago, Sammy slammed his 48th homer in the fifth inning, passing McGwire for the first time. Three innings later, Mark knocked his 48th, tying the score; and then, in the 10th, Big Mac parked the game winner beyond the center-field wall to reclaim the top spot*

As this chase moved apace, the entire baseball-speaking world was abuzz with words long uncoupled: Babe and Roger, Hack and Mac, race and record. *Everybody was talking baseball,* and two men dominated the discussion. Mark and Sammy. Sammy and Mark.

13

Every morning fans and neighbors would reach for some news-gathering outlet or ask a fellow commuter, How did So-and-so do last night? What about Mac-and-such? ◆ We rooted for these most gracious, genuine and grounded of rivals who seemed to take such pleasure in the sport (and each other), and who generously expended time and money on folks blessed with less.

Who could choose a favorite when even they themselves could not? ◆ *Sammy:* "I'm rooting for Mac." ◆ *Mac:* "Wouldn't it be great if we just ended up tied?" ◆ If we couldn't pick a winner, we certainly would watch and wonder: Can they keep up the pace? Who will drop off the pace? What if they both exceed all previous paces? ◆ Mac had always said the same thing about *his* pace—that if he had 50 by the final month, "I'd have a shot."

On September 1, Mac fired off his 56th and 57th, smashing *Hack Wilson's* 68-year-old National League single-season mark (followed, three days later, by Sammy smoking Hack's Cub record with his 57th).

On September 8, in the fourth inning at home against Chicago, after joyously rounding the bases for the 62nd time and lifting the historic moment even higher with emotional hugs to son, Matt, and newfound friend Sammy Sosa, Mark McGwire clambered into the stands to embrace the grown children of Roger Maris.

62
What could top this?

In a single swipe, the untouchable 61 by Roger Maris that

stood for 37 years took a seat to an even more mighty,

mythical and magical number. Within the same week—can

you stand this pace?—Sammy Sosa reached out and tapped

his 62 into the books (while, in another city, McGwire sent

his love). The Cubs' Wild Card duel with the Mets added even

more suspense to the thrilling two-man sprint to the finish.

Then, in a blink of a slugger's eye,

this extraordinary baseball year was over.

History. Cooperstown-bound.

The race for the single-season home run record had a winner. The place next to the new number, 70, had a name: Mark McGwire. As the glory and celebration of his reign begins, we praise and thank both Mark and Sammy for all the singular moments and memories. (Was it just one season?) These heroes reached unrivaled heights and took us along for an unparalleled ride. We wish them an equal measure of pleasure, satisfaction and peace in their accomplishments. Sammy Sosa and Mark McGwire kept their own sweet, frenetic time, moving at a pace unseen and unmatched in baseball history.

Remember

If you lined up every hitter who ever contended for the home run title in any season spanning more than a century of Major League play, you'd count only 17 men who ever reached the slugger's standard of 50 — only 26 times.

Now, raise the mark many notches to the monumental boundary of 60, and you'll **find a mere four players** beyond that line—four very different men—who converged from scattering winds in this rarefied air: 1. George Herman "Babe" Ruth, from the East, the Yankee who broke the single-season home run record (27, established by Ned Williamson of the Cubs in 1884) with 29 in 1919, and then shattered it again (54 in 1920) and again (59 in 1921) before staking the summit (60 in 1927) that would stand for 34 years; 2. Midwesterner Roger Maris, who one-upped his fellow Yankee with his 61 homers in '61; and now, 37 seasons later, both 3. Mark McGwire, from out West, and 4. Sammy Sosa, from the Dominican Republic, surpassing Maris and making their mark.

EDWARD N. WILLIAMSON,
CHICAGO CLUB, THIRD BASE.

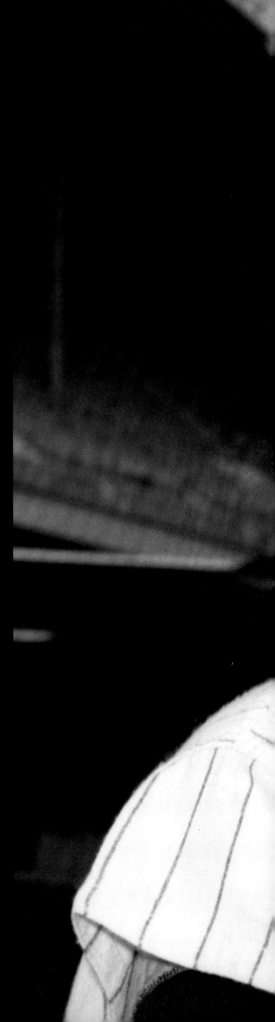

An even *finer line* of intertwining similarities, connections and coincidences can be tightly drawn around this heroic quartet:

- *Roger Maris* hit his first home run of the 1961 season—a grand slam—in the fifth inning. *Mark McGwire* hit his first home run of the 1998 season—a grand slam—in the fifth inning.

- *Maris* broke *Babe Ruth's* record 13 years after the Babe died in 1948. *McGwire* broke *Maris's* record 13 years after Roger passed away in 1985.

- *McGwire* was born on October 1, 1963, two years to the day after *Maris* broke Ruth's 34-year-old record.

Babe Ruth began his pro career as a pitcher (compiling a 94–46 record with Boston). *Mark McGwire* began his college career as a pitcher at USC. (Ned Williamson appeared as a pitcher in 7 of his 13 big-league seasons, all but one year with the Chicago Cubs.)

 Babe Ruth, Roger Maris and *Sammy Sosa* were all exceptional right fielders throughout their careers.

Babe Ruth, Roger Maris and *Sammy Sosa* each had two daughters.

 Mark McGwire has one son (just under 11 years old). *Sammy Sosa* has four children (whose ages total just under 11 years old).

Babe Ruth's record-breaking 60th home run ball was caught by hometown (New York) resident *Joe Forner. Mark McGwire's* record-breaking 62nd home run ball was caught by hometown (St. Louis) resident *Tim Forneris*.

For his 60th home run, *McGwire* hit an infrared-coded ball marked with the number 3 (the *Babe's* jersey number) on the third pitch, becoming only the third man in history to pass that mark. (Cincy pitchers had thrown 33 prior pitches to him during the series.)

McGwire hit his 61st homer on September 7, 1998, his father's 61st birthday (three days before what would have been Roger Maris's 64th birthday).

McGwire hit home run 62 a day before the Pick–3 lottery number in St. Louis was 062, while the temperature (at least in New York) was 62 degrees.

50-HOMER CLUB

1920	Babe Ruth	Yankees	54
1921	Babe Ruth	Yankees	59
1927	Babe Ruth	Yankees	60
1928	Babe Ruth	Yankees	54
1930	Hack Wilson	Cubs	56
1932	Jimmie Foxx	Athletics	58
1938	Hank Greenberg	Tigers	58
1938	Jimmie Foxx	Red Sox	50
1947	Ralph Kiner	Pirates	51
1947	Johnny Mize	Giants	51
1949	Ralph Kiner	Pirates	54
1955	Willie Mays	Giants	51
1956	Mickey Mantle	Yankees	52
1961	Roger Maris	Yankees	61
1965	Willie Mays	Giants	52
1977	George Foster	Reds	52
1990	Cecil Fielder	Tigers	51
1995	Albert Belle	Indians	50
1996	Mark McGwire	Athletics	52
1996	Brady Anderson	Orioles	50
1997	Mark McGwire	A's/Cards	58
1997	Ken Griffey, Jr.	Mariners	56
1998	Ken Griffey, Jr.	Mariners	56
1998	Mark McGwire	Cardinals	70
1998	Sammy Sosa	Cubs	66
1998	Greg Vaughn	Padres	50

60-HOMER CLUB

1927	Babe Ruth	Yankees	60
1961	Roger Maris	Yankees	61
1998	Mark McGwire	Cardinals	70
1998	Sammy Sosa	Cubs	66

70-HOMER CLUB

1998	Mark McGwire	Cardinals	70

THIS SPECIAL SEASON

31

Mark McGwire and Ken Griffey, Jr., who ranked first and second in Major League home runs last season with 58 and 56, respectively, both smack Opening Day roundtrippers. McGwire's 354-foot grand slam off Ramon Martinez in the fifth sparks the Cardinals home win over the Dodgers, 6 – 0. Griffey's 404-foot solo shot off Charles Nagy in the fifth gives the Mariners a 4-3 lead before they fall, 10-9, to the Indians.

April

4 With his fourth consecutive long-ball in as many days, Big Mac ties the record held by Willie Mays.

14 Against the Arizona Diamondbacks, Mac becomes the first Cardinal to go deep three times in a game at Busch Stadium.

MAJOR LEAGUE HOME RUN LEADERS

Vinny Castilla, Colorado (N)	11
Ken Griffey, Jr., Seattle (A)	11
Mark McGwire, St. Louis (N)	11
Andres Galarraga, Atlanta (N)	10
Chipper Jones, Atlanta (N)	9
Dean Palmer, Kansas City (A)	9
Alex Rodriguez, Seattle (A)	9

8 After giving up McGwire's 400th career circuit clout at Shea Stadium, right-hander Rick Reed says of the relatively paltry 358-foot distance the ball traveled: "He hit it a mile high, and it looked like a pop-up. But it kept going . . . 800 feet in the air, and it landed in the first row of seats."

16 McGwire hits the longest homer ever recorded in Busch Stadium history (and his career) with a 545-foot solo blast, soon commemorated with a four-foot Band-Aid.

25 Sammy Sosa, heretofore missing from the tater leader board, hits his 11th of the year—a 3-run, 420-foot shot—kicking off a ferocious tear in which he will whack a record 21 dingers in a 30-day span (22 games).

With his 25th four-bagger in St. Louis, McGwire breaks the Major League record for most homers totaled before June 1.

30 Mac homers in San Diego, the 16th time he's gone deep in May, setting a new team record for the month.

MAJOR LEAGUE HOME RUN LEADERS

Mark McGwire, St. Louis (N)	27
Alex Rodriguez, Seattle (A)	20
Vinny Castilla, Colorado (N)	19
Andres Galarraga, Atlanta (N)	19
Ken Griffey, Jr., Seattle (A)	19
Jose Canseco, Toronto (A)	17
Juan Gonzalez, Texas (A)	17
Greg Vaughn, San Diego (N)	17

June

1 Sammy starts slammin' with a 2-run, 430-foot shot (his 14th of the season) in Wrigley against the Marlins in the first inning, then socks a 3-run, 410-footer in the eighth.

7 Sammy completes a scorching Interleague series at home by knocking his third roundtripper in three straight days against the crosstown White Sox.

12 Mac smashes his 11th career grand slam (and 2nd of '98) with a 438-foot drive (his 31st big fly of the year) in Arizona.

17 Big Red smacks his first roundtripper in the Houston Astrodome, a 438-foot solo wallop.

20 Sammy's second home run of the day, a 500-foot blast off Philadelphia's Toby Borland, ties the league mark for most dingers (8) in any calendar week (June 14–20).

30 Slammin' Sammy Sosa's grand slam in the eighth inning, his 20th in June (33rd overall), sets a Major League record for most in any month.

Big Mac's 37th clout ties the Major League record for most HRs heading into the All-Star Break.

MAJOR LEAGUE HOME RUN LEADERS
Mark McGwire, St. Louis (N) 37
Ken Griffey, Jr., Seattle (A) 33
Sammy Sosa, Chicago (N) 33
Andres Galarraga, Atlanta (N) 27
Alex Rodriguez, Seattle (A) 27
Greg Vaughn, San Diego (N) 27
Jose Canseco, Toronto (A) 24
Juan Gonzalez, Texas (A) 24
Rafael Palmiero, Baltimore (A) 24

J U L Y

6 The day before the All-Star Game in Colorado, Sammy Sosa is sitting with his friend, Ken Griffey, Jr., in an interview room beneath Coors Field when he's asked who (he, McGwire or Griffey) has the best chance of breaking Maris's record 61 homers this season. "I have my money on Mark McGwire," he says, smiling. "Griffey, I know you my boy, but ..." All three are on pace to surpass Maris's record.

12 Big Mac's two big knocks at home against the Astros mark the fastest a Major Leaguer has ever reached 40 four-baggers in a season—in both at-bats (281) and games (90).

26 McGwire's 44th home run, a 452-foot moon shot launched at Coors Field, establishes a new St. Louis Cardinals single-season milestone, eclipsing the 43 that Johnny Mize posted in 1940.

27 Sosa's 438-foot grand salami in Arizona (his 40th season dinger) marks the first grand slam of his 10-year Major League career.

28 Getting the hang of this grand slam thing, Sammy leaves the same yard, again with all bags juiced.

MAJOR LEAGUE HOME RUN LEADERS

Mark McGwire, St. Louis (N) 45

Sammy Sosa, Chicago (N) 42

Ken Griffey, Jr., Seattle (A) 41

Greg Vaughn, San Diego (N) 38

Vinny Castilla, Colorado (N) 35

Albert Belle, Chicago (A) 33

Andres Galarraga, Atlanta (N) 33

Rafael Palmiero, Baltimore (A) 33

10 Sammy smacks a couple of solo shots in San Francisco for numbers 45 and 46 (to tie him with Mac).

11 Mac hits No. 47, the most ever by a National Leaguer prior to September 1.

19 In a head-to-head matchup against McGwire and his Cardinals in Chicago, Sosa leaves the yard for the 48th time, taking the dinger lead for the first time all year (and setting a single-season record for most home runs by a Latin American ballplayer). McGwire trails Sosa for three innings before knocking his 48th clear out of Wrigley Field in the eighth to tie the game and, two innings later, reclaims the tater supremacy (and leads his team to an 8–6 victory).

A U G U S T

20 After blasting his 50th (the first man to reach at least 50 in three consecutive seasons), Mac thrusts his fist into the air and claps his hands twice as he rounds the bases. Says Cards skipper Tony La Russa: "Never have I seen him show more emotion than that on the field." St. Louis batting practice pitcher Dave McKay says that Mac and he had "never talked about 62. We've always talked about 50. That was big for him." After hitting his 51st in the second game of the double-dip with the Mets, McGwire finally admits: "I'd have to say I do have a shot."

22 Mac attacks three records with his 52nd: He (1) sets Major League milestone with 162 home runs over three straight seasons; (2) becomes first player in history to accumulate 52 before September 1; (3) surpasses National League mark for first basemen.

23 Lost in the hoopla over the two-man duel is the milestone reached by Barry Bonds, who becomes the first Major League ballplayer to hit 400 home runs and steal 400 bases in a career. Bonds, who's usually in the thick of tater-top country, says he's as caught up in the home run race as everyone else: "Hey, you've got a chance to break a record that no one thought would ever be broken," says Bonds. "So, I'm watching it, too . . . I'm watching the home run derby."

31 With his 55th knock, clocked at home against the Reds, Sammy catches Mark again.

MAJOR LEAGUE HOME RUN LEADERS

Player	HR
Mark McGwire, St. Louis (N)	55
Sammy Sosa, Chicago (N)	55
Ken Griffey, Jr., Seattle (A)	47
Greg Vaughn, San Diego (N)	45
Andres Galarraga, Atlanta (N)	42
Albert Belle, Chicago (A)	41
Rafael Palmiero, Baltimore (A)	41

1 When Florida fans playfully boo him for hitting just a single in the third inning, Big Mac laughs: "I hope they understand this is not an easy task." Before the game ends, he will show them—and us—how easy he can make it look, **leading off the seventh with a 450-foot blast**, and then launching one 22 feet farther in the ninth, breaking Hack Wilson's 1930 National League record of 56 set with the Cubs. "They looked **like Ping-Pong balls** going out," says Marlins manager Jim Leyland. "I've never seen anything like it."

⚾ Greg Vaughn hits his 46th and 47th in New York, giving him three in two nights, and seven in his last 10 games. *2* Sosa ties Wilson's 68-year-old Cubs record in Chicago. A picture of Hack Wilson happens to hang next to Sosa's locker, accompanied by his final interview that includes these words: "**Talent isn't enough**. You need common sense and good advice." ⚾ For the second straight day, McGwire hits two against the Marlins (the first, a 497-footer into the upper deck in left, is the third longest in Pro Player Stadium history); the **45,170 fans** demand a curtain call both times. Mac: "I've said time and time again, I wish every player could have that feeling." *4* Sosa hits number 57 (his first off a Pittsburgh hurler this season), breaking Wilson's Cub record, and says of McGwire: "I think he'll break [Maris's record] this weekend." ⚾ Though he goes **homerless against the Reds**, McGwire presents St. Louis personnel with a memento. "When I arrived at my locker today," says pitcher Kent Bottenfield, "there was a signed ball by Mark [commemorating] his [NL-record] 57th home run. He did that for all his teammates. **He's just a great guy**." ⚾ Mac had one day off in these two weeks—and spent ten hours filming a public-service announcement, paid for by him, on child abuse, a charity to which he donates $1 million a year and countless hours.

September 5 After the Cardinals unveil a statue of Stan (the original "Man") Musial, who plays "Take Me Out to the Ballgame" on his harmonica at home plate in a red sports coat and red shoes, Mac becomes the third man in Major League history to hit 60 home runs in a single season. "I mean, geez, Babe Ruth," he says. "What can you say? Geez. You're almost speechless when people put your name alongside his name." Deni Allen, a 22-year-old fan, returns the historic ball to McGwire after the game, saying: "It's his ball . . . It would've burned a hole in my heart if I had hung on to it." ⚾ Seven hours after Mac hits his 60th, Sammy Sosa clocks his 58th, but his Cubs fall short to Pittsburgh, 4–3. **September 7** "It's going to be electrifying," says McGwire of the final Cards-Cubs series in St. Louis. "If you can't be looking forward to these two games, then your heart isn't beating." ⚾ In the pregame press conference, Mac and Sammy sip bottled water and swap one-liners, seeming to enjoy every moment of their elite company. "Wouldn't it be great if we just ended up tied?" Mac asks. "I think it would be beautiful." What number? "Seventy is a good one." "I will take it," Sammy agrees. ⚾ On this Labor Day, the 61st birthday of Mark McGwire's father (both of his parents are in the stands, as well as four of Roger Maris's sons and two daughters—their mother is hospitalized for a "heart flutter"), the

34-year-old first baseman slams his 61st at 1:21 p.m. Central time on Mike Morgan's third pitch in the first inning. Raising his arms exultantly, he trots around the bases, giddy as a Little Leaguer. At home, with those huge arms, he scoops his son, Matt, off the ground. (Manager Tony La Russa says: "I will get a picture of that. It's the damnedest thing

I've seen in the big leagues.") In his curtain call, he touches a few more bases: wishing his father a "happy birthday," saluting Sosa and the crowd with Sammy-like kisses and, in homage to the man he just tied, pointing at the Maris family and patting his heart. In the eighth, after Sosa singles to left, the two men embrace at first base. "Now you have to wait for me," Sammy says. "Don't go too fast."

After the game, Mac says: "I don't think I'll ever let go of the moment . . . I know that I am one swing away. You know, the whole time I just thought, What a great birthday present for my father." ⚾ Mike Davidson, the fan who wins the scramble for No. 61, says he plans to return the ball to McGwire: "It will mean more to him and baseball than it will for me." ⚾ A few hours after McGwire blasts his 61st, Ken Griffey, Jr., reaches 50 with his second of a game against Baltimore, making this the first season ever in which three men hit at least 50 homers.

September 8 At the age of 10, Mark McGwire homered in his first ever Little League at-bat, a line shot over the right-field fence. He couldn't wait to tell his parents, but they were off on a cruise and wouldn't be home for a week. ⚾ Today, Mark McGwire hits his legend-making 62nd home run of this season and runs around the bases with the joy of a little boy. He wouldn't have to wait long to share it with his parents: they're seated right behind home plate. ⚾ Prior to the game, Mac meets with the six Maris children, who show him the bat with which their late father had hit his 61st on October 1, 1961. "Now I can honestly say my bat will lie next to his [in the Hall of Fame]," McGwire says. In the fourth inning, with two outs, Mac takes his own bat off the rack and whacks Steve Trachsel's first pitch inches over the left-field wall, beyond any other Major Leaguer in history. **September 11** After going five games without a dinger, Sosa sails his 59th over and out of Wrigley Field and onto Sheffield Avenue in a tough loss to the Brewers, 13–11. **September 12** Sammy slams number 60, driving a seventh-inning pitch 430 feet from home plate and clear out of his home park (and tying him with the Babe's once unassailable landmark). More good news for Cub fans: with their 15–12 slugfest win over the Brewers, and the Mets 5–3 loss to the Expos, Chicago holds a one-game lead in the National League Wild Card race. **September 13** Knocking on the new ceiling recently installed by his buddy Mac, Sammy hammers out a 480-foot 61st in the fifth inning, then blasts through to the 62nd level (and again onto the streets of Chicago) with another 480-footer. Once more the Cubs win (in 10 innings, 11–10)! Cubs win! Sammy hits 62!

15 As a **ninth-inning** pinch-hitter, McGwire goes deep for #63. **16** Sammy smacks his 63rd with a game-winning **grand slam** (his third base-juiced knock of the season). **17** Ken Griffey, Jr., rips his 53rd home run in **Oakland**, **one day after** becoming the third Major Leaguer ever to **reach 50** homers and 20 steals in a season. **18** Mac **whacks** his 64th in Milwaukee.

19 Dominican-born Cleveland outfielder Manny Ramirez hits two homers against the Royals (his 44th and 45th), tying him for the Major League record with eight dingers in his last five games. ● Seattle shortstop Alex Rodriguez becomes only the third Major Leaguer to register 40 home runs and 40 stolen bases in a season. ● Texas's Juan Gonzalez is the 81st man to hit 300 career homers (the sixth-youngest, in the sixth-fewest at-bats, ever). **20** Mark makes good on a preseason promise to his son, Matt, by clouting his 65th homer in the first inning at Milwaukee, but just misses out on number 66 when his fifth-inning liner—landing near the yellow line in left—is ruled a double.

On **Sammy Sosa Day** in Chicago, the Dominican-American right fielder is honored by **dignitaries** from his native and adopted nations and showered with gifts and affection from family, friends, colleagues, and **40,117** fans.

23 Sosa breaks out of an 0-for-21 slump with a **big bang**—make that two huge bangs—by slamming numeros 64 and 65 (tying Mac) in **Milwaukee**, but the Cubbies **blow** a 7-0 lead and lose, 8-7; with the Mets loss, they remain tied for the **Wild Card** lead.

25 The final-weekend **fireworks** kick off at 8:54 p.m. ET with Sammy Sosa's 66th blast in Houston, **matched** 45 minutes later by Mark McGwire! Cubs, Mets lose; Giants victory earns them a three-way **Wild Card** tie. Ken Griffey, Jr., matches last year's career-high tater total of 56.

26 Top this!! Big Mac whacks **two more** big jacks against the Expos in St. Louis for a season total of 68 home runs! ("I just want everyone to have **fun** this weekend.") Slammin' Sammy's two singles help the Cubs win! ("Yesterday I hit a home run and we **lost**. Today I got two hits and we **won**. I feel better today.")

27 Topping off the last scheduled day of the regular season, Mark McGwire goes deep for the 69th time! In the home seventh, at 3:20 p.m. CT, Big Mac takes his final swing on the first pitch from Montreal pitcher Carl Pavano. Boom! A cannon shot clears the left-field fence for number 70. Seventy!! ⚾ San Diego's Greg Vaughn becomes the fourth member of the 50-homer club; previously, there'd never been more than two players in a season. ⚾ Mets lose to Atlanta, 7–2, ending their playoff hopes. In Houston, Sammy Sosa singles in Chicago's first run (his 158th Major League-leading RBI), but the Astros come back to win in 11 innings, 4–3. Minutes later, Colorado's Neifi Perez homers in the bottom of the ninth, capping an 0-7 comeback against the Giants, 9-8. So, this glorious season goes another day: a one-game playoff in Chicago, Cubs vs. Giants, for the Wild Card berth.

28 The Cubs defeat the Giants. Sammy is held to a pair of singles to finish at 66 home runs, four behind McGwire.

FINAL MAJOR LEAGUE HOME RUN STANDINGS

Mark McGwire, St. Louis (N) 70
Sammy Sosa, Chicago (N) 66
Ken Griffey, Jr., Seattle (A) 56
Greg Vaughn, San Diego (N) 50
Albert Belle, Chicago (A) 49
Vinny Castilla, Colorado (N) 46
Jose Canseco, Toronto (A) 46
Manny Ramirez, Cleveland (A) 45
Andres Galarraga, Atlanta (N) 44

SIXTY-TWO/SIXTY-TWO

The Man: **Mark David McGwire**

Age: **34**

Birth Date: **10/1/63**

Birthplace: **Pomona, California**

Height: **6 feet, 5 inches**

Weight: **255 pounds**

Position: **First baseman**

Number: **25**

Team: **St. Louis Cardinals**

Nicknames: **Mac, Big Mac**

Marital Status: **Divorced (good friends with ex-wife and her husband), one son (Matt)**

Date: **September 8, 1998**

Place: **St. Louis, Missouri**

Teams: **Chicago Cubs vs. St. Louis Cardinals**

Attendance: **49,987**

Heartfelt Moment: **Before the game, Hall of Fame officials hand Mac the Louisville Slugger with which Roger Maris hit his 61st homer in 1961. "Roger, I hope you are with me tonight," Mac says, rubbing the bat on his chest. "I touched the bat with my heart."**

Fair Exchange: Deni Allen, who bartered McGwire's 60th home run ball in return for some Mac memorabilia and 15 minutes of batting practice, takes his cuts with the Cards, stroking a few near the warning track.

Countdown: Cubs lead, 2–0, in the fourth (two outs, no one on) when Steve Trachsel delivers the first pitch to McGwire at 9:18 p.m. EDT.

Distance: 341 feet (Mac's shortest home run of '98 season).

Location: The ball travels on a screaming line drive just beyond the eight-foot left-field wall. ◆ *Finder No-Keeper:* "Mr. McGwire, I found something that belongs to you," says 22-year-old groundskeeper Tim Forneris upon returning the historic baseball to the man who "just lost it." ◆ *Display Items:* In addition to the ball, Mark McGwire's bat and full uniform (cap, jersey, cleats, batting gloves), bat boy Matt McGwire's uniform, and radio announcer Jack Buck's scorecard are shipped to the Baseball Hall of Fame for immediate exhibition. ◆

First (Off) Base: Dave McKay, first-base coach and batting-practice pitcher (who estimates giving up 8,000 dingers to Mac in B.P.), gently reminds his charge to touch 'em all after a brief stumble over the bag.

Father and Son: After trading high-fives and even hugs with Cub infielders, Mac is mobbed at home by teammates and then picks up his bat boy son, Matt, high in the air. ◆ *Mano a Mano:* Sammy Sosa, who trots in from right field to congratulate his friendly rival, is also lifted in a bear hug by "the man." ◆ *Touching Tribute:* Mac climbs into the stands near the first-base dugout (right) to embrace each of Roger and Pat Maris's six children.

Mac says over the public-address system: "To all my family, my son, the Cubs, Sammy Sosa, **it's unbelievable!** Thank you, St. Louis!"

Time of Celebration: Eleven minutes. ◆ *What a Ride:* After 6–3 win over Cubs, Big Mac and son Matt, seated in backseat of '62 Cardinal-red Corvette convertible presented by team, wave to the 40,000 fans still cheering an hour after the game. ◆ *Mac's Post-Game Quote #1:* "I can honestly say now that I can rest my bat alongside Roger Maris's bat in the Hall of Fame." ◆ *Mac's Post-Game Quote #2:* "I hope someday my son grows up to be a baseball player and breaks the record."

The Man: *Samuel Peralta Sosa ("Mark's the man in America. I'm the man in the Dominican.")*

Age: *29*

Birth Date: *11/10/68*

Birthplace: *San Pedro de Macoris, Dominican Republic*

Height: *6 feet*

Weight: *200 pounds*

Position: *Right fielder*

Number: *21*

Team: *Chicago Cubs*

Nickname: *Slammin' Sammy*

Marital Status: *Married (Sonia), four children (Keisha, Kenia, Sammy, Jr., Michael)*

Date: *September 13, 1998*

Place: *Chicago, Illinois*

Teams: *Milwaukee Brewers vs. Chicago Cubs*

Attendance: *40,846*

First Pitch: *In the fifth inning, Sammy hits an 0–1 fast ball off Bronswell Patrick for his 61st home run of the season.*

Distance: 480 feet. ◆ *Location:* The ball soars over Wrigley Field's left-field fence, skipping across Waveland Avenue and down Kenmore. ◆ *Heartfelt Moment:* After rounding diamond and hugging teammates, Sammy flashes trademark salute (thumps heart with hand, blows two-fingered kisses, makes V sign) and turns to camera. "I love you, Mama," he says. ◆ Bigger Pitch: Sammy's historic 62nd home run (a solo shot) off Eric Plunk's 2–1 fastball in the ninth inning, at 4:44 Central time, triggers a game-tying rally (Cubs win, 11–10, in 10th). ◆ *Distance:* 480 feet. ◆ Location: The ball sails over the friendly confines' left-center-field wall onto Waveland Avenue and bounces down an alley. ◆ *Reaction Shot:* On the heels of his patented leap-skip of exultation, with no more show than fists clenched, Slammin' Sammy runs around the bases as if it's a routine homer. ◆ *Fan Chants:* "Sam-mee! Sam-mee!", "So-sa! So-sa!" and "M-V-P! M-V-P!" ◆ *Curtain Calls:* Three.

Time of Celebration: Six minutes. ◆ ***Mother and Son:***

Eyes filling with tears, Sammy blows kisses to his mother,

Mireya, who's watching back home in Santo Domingo. ◆

Amigo a Amigo: After the game, as he fluidly and fluently

conducts interviews in English and Spanish, Sammy sends his

best to Mark McGwire: "I wish you could be here with me

today." ◆ ***Sammy's Post-Game Quote #1:*** For the record

Sammy exclaims, "It's unbelievable! I have to say what I did is

for the people of Chicago, for America, for my mother, for my

wife, my kids, and the people I have around me." ◆ ***Sammy's***

Post-Game Quote #2: "They must be dancing in the streets in

Santo Domingo. Maybe I will do a little dance myself tonight."

◆ ***Sammy's Post-Game Quote #3:*** "I feel great to be

there with Babe Ruth, Roger Maris, and Mark McGwire."

TOUCH 'EM ALL

Tater. Dinger. Long-ball. Roundtripper. Four-bagger. Circuit clout. Going deep. Going yard. Parking it. Elvis has left the building. Knock. Big knock. Big fly. Big salami.

Roger Maris liked to call it the "big tonk."

◆   The home run can't be confined within a baseball field or contained by a single appellation.

◆   The home run transcends baseball ("You hit a home run with that report, Fenster . . . ").

◆   The home run is perhaps the most exciting moment in sports.

◆   The home run is baseball's signature feat.

◆   The home run appeals to our roots of rugged individualism.

◆   The home run affirms our fascination with grand scale.

◆   "The home run is a form of dominance people want to see." (Jim Riggleman, Cubs manager)

The home run must be hit within "a certain number of turns in a season . . . whereas in other sports you can achieve records more easily by deciding to do so, giving the ball to a running back to gain a record number of yards or giving a player enough shots in basketball so he can score a certain number of points" (Steve Hirdt, statistician). "Home runs are the easiest things to count, not to mention admire." (Bob Costas, sportscaster) The home run record (single-season) is the most revered and renowned record in sports. The home run record was the first to get people interested in records. "The home run record's mystique is enhanced because of who set it first: Babe Ruth." (Costas)

THE BABE

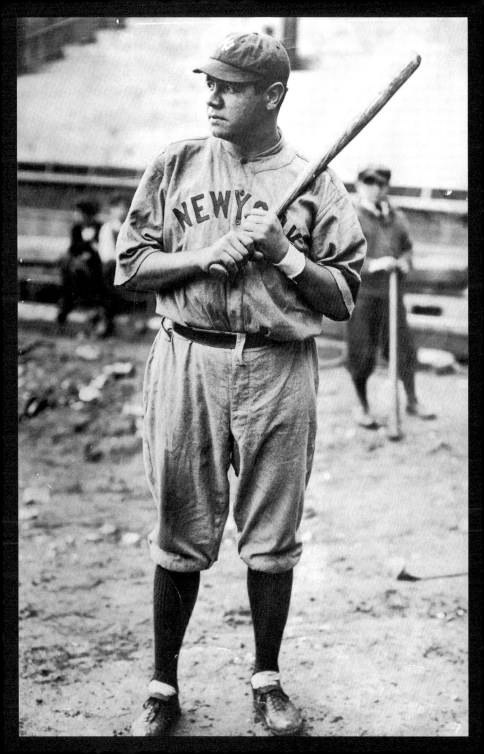

In **1916**, as a **southpaw pitcher** with the Red Sox, George Herman Ruth won 23 games, topping the league in **shutouts** (9), ERA (1.75) and opponents' batting average (.201). ◆ It was with a bat in his hands, however, that he became the **legendary** Babe. The Bambino. The Sultan of Swat. At a time when Major League "sluggers" were barely reaching double figures in **home runs**, the Babe came along and dominated—decimated—the competition. ◆ What competition? ◆ Babe Ruth **hit 29** four-baggers in 1919 (after tying for the Major League lead with 11 the previous year), nearly **tripling** the total of the nearest American Leaguer (Tilly Walker, with 10), and in the following season, wearing **Yankee pinstripes**, the Bambino moved beyond mortal barriers and swatted 54 roundtrippers, while league runner-up George Sisler (19) and National League leader Cy Williams (14) were the men who would be **home run king**.

Babe Ruth still holds the record for most years leading the majors in **home runs** (12). ◆ Babe Ruth, now second to Henry Aaron (755) on the all-time home run list with 714, still ranks ahead of all **left-handed batters**. ◆ There are so many more marks and numbers still attached to his name. Babe Ruth was the **greatest** ballplayer of his era, probably of all time. But his impact is **incalculable**. More than 100 years after his birth, and 50 years after he proved mortal—withered and weakened by cancer—he remains **bigger than life**: arguably the biggest sports figure in history, and one of the biggest **influences** on **twentieth-century** American culture.

Babe was—and is—a **giant** of a man. Everything he did was MORE. ◆ MUCH more. ◆ He left nothing on the **field** and, away from the **diamond**, gave everything else a helluva run. He was a big, **flamboyant** man playing in the media capital who lived up to (and transcended) his **legend**. ◆ Which is why we found this season's home run race so **compelling**. Two great players (Mark McGwire and Sammy Sosa) chasing two other great players (Babe and Roger Maris), one of whom was the **greatest**. ◆ In his day—in fact, on the exact day that he set the single- season **home run** record—the big, boisterous Babe, celebrating in the **clubhouse** with his teammates, boasted to everyone within earshot: "Sixty, count 'em, **sixty!**" And then the dare: "Let's see some other [fellow] match that!" ◆ Well, big fellow, **34 years later**, one daring man did just that. . . .

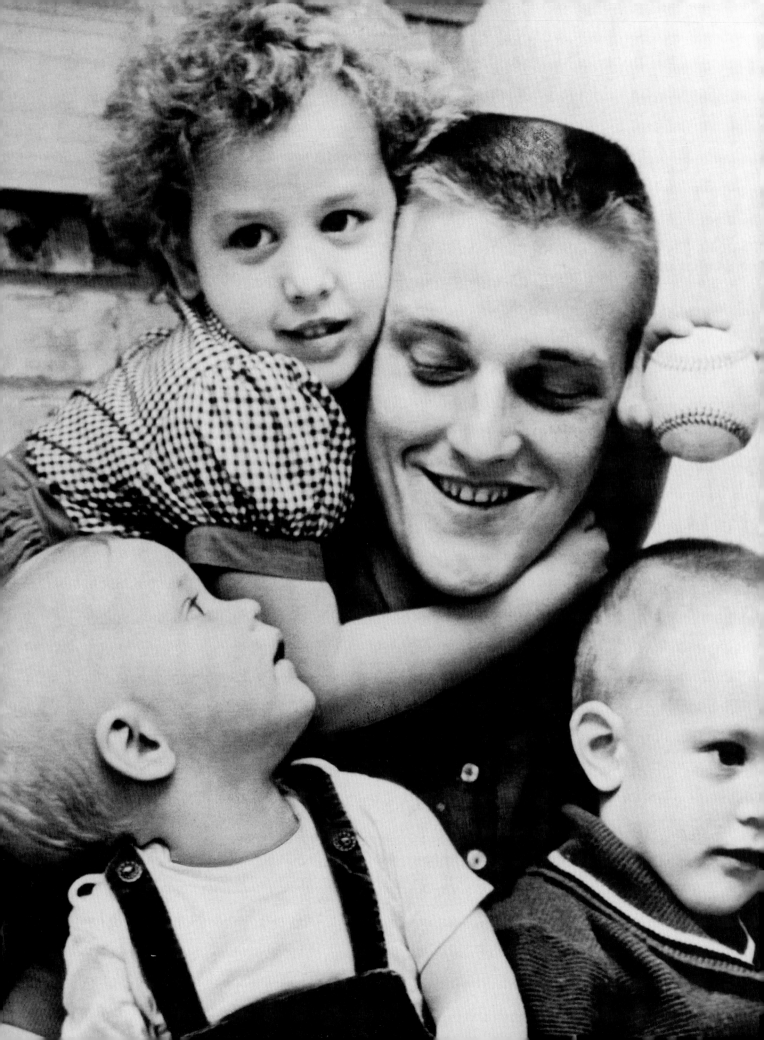

The man who not only matched but beat Babe's **larger-than-life** single-season home run record was "the most reserved, quiet individual I ever knew" (according to his Yankee teammate Bobby Richardson), as distant in temperament from the Bambino as North Dakota is unlike New York. ◆ Roger Maris was, to the end of his days, a **man of few words**. No Babe, no Bambino, no Sultan of Swat . . . he had no real lasting nickname at all. If you had to describe this **reluctant hero**, you would probably begin with those two words: North Dakota. He was an honest, tough, spare, **hardworking** fellow born with terrific tools but uncomfortable bragging about them. In the heat and glare of the **spotlight**, he tended to shrink in discomfort. He just wanted to do his job. ◆ In 1961, his job was to turn on a pitch, **swing** from the left-handed side and drive the ball out of the stadium. He also had other tasks, which he performed as well as any ballplayer of his day: he could field his position and throw with power and **accuracy** (Whitey Herzog said, "You couldn't play right field any better than Roger did"), as well as run the bases with

speed and intelligence. ◆ Though many baseball fans knew of his skills—he had won the American League **Most Valuable Player** Award in 1960 (.283 batting average, 39 homers, with a league-best 112 RBI and .581 slugging percentage)—to most folks he remained a mystery. ◆ Seeming to come out of nowhere, his name and face were **suddenly splashed** all over the newspapers and magazines and on television. Invariably, he was seen with—and compared to—the Babe, who held the most revered record in sports (the one Roger was now pursuing with all his heart, drive and quiet grit). ◆ Mike Shannon, a former roommate of Maris's with the Cardinals and now a broadcaster, says that Roger was "the kind of guy you really liked to be around and happy to call your friend . . . a very kind, gentle, caring person who happens to have a **tremendous** amount of ability to play baseball." Dick Young, the late New York sportswriter, said: "I thought Roger was a **helluva guy**, the way he handled the press down the stretch in 1961. The thing to remember is that new newspapermen were joining the pack every day. Many of the questions

were the same ones he'd heard day after day, and I kept waiting for Roger to blow his top . . . But he didn't. He just sat there, propped in his locker . . . answering them." ◆ After **Maris hit his 60th** home run, he told reporters: "I was in a complete daze. I couldn't believe what happened. Had I really hit 60 home runs? Had I **tied Babe Ruth** for the highest total ever hit in a season?" On 2:43 Sunday afternoon, October 1, 1961, before a roaring crowd of 23,154 in Yankee Stadium (the "House That Ruth Built"), 27-year-old Roger Maris **stroked number 61** in the fourth inning off 24-year-old Boston rookie Tracy Stallard. It dropped into the lower right-field stands, 10 rows deep and 10 feet from the bullpen, **365 feet from home**. Reluctant to take his "bow" for the fans, he literally had to be pushed out of the dugout by his teammates. ◆ There were no boasts from the **new home run king**, only a sense of enormous relief, pride and satisfaction. ◆ It was the response of a North Dakota man whose tombstone in Fargo bears this simple inscription: **Against All Odds**.

THE LONG WAY HOME

A splitter catches

the black of the plate. A squibbler skips past a fielder's glove. A screaming liner **ticks the top of the fence.**

Baseball has always been a game of inches. **This incredible year, Mark McGwire and Sammy Sosa stepped up big-time** to push way beyond any previous measure **of performance.** Mark McGwire's rainmakers flew so high and deep that such lofty subjects as physics and calculus were invariably brought into play: His 16th home run on May 16, for example, was calculated at 545 feet, the longest homer ever recorded in Busch Stadium history (and Mac's career), while other shots fell roughly 500 (#55), 510 (#42 and #54), and 527 (#14) feet from home plate. If all of Mac's 70 home runs were strung together, they would reach nearly 5-1/2 miles. Some distances, of course, can't be measured in feet, yards, or even miles. Take Sammy Sosa's journey from the rough-hewn streets (where he washed cars, sold oranges, and shined shoes) and fields (where he played baseball with a rolled-up sock for a ball, a tree branch for a bat, and a milk carton for a glove) of San Pedro de Macoris in the Dominican Republic. In 1996, Sammy helped build a shopping center there. In the middle of the plaza is a fountain flowing into a wishing well for coin-sent dreams (the money all goes to charity), as well as a statue of Sosa in his Cubs uniform. The inscription reads(in Spanish): FOUNTAIN OF THE SHOE-SHINE BOYS. More recently, Sammy established a charitable foundation to help hurricane victims in his homeland. Mark has long funded a foundation for abused children. Both men know well that the long way home seems shorter when you can share the load. In 1927, the great Babe Ruth had the great Lou Gehrig batting behind him, even matching him homer for homer through August. "I don't think I ever would have established my home run record of 60 if it hadn't been for Lou," Babe said. In 1961, the M & M boys were also Yankee teammates protecting each other in the lineup (and off the field as well), until Mickey Mantle fell off the pace with a leg injury (and 54 dingers), while it was left to Roger Maris to soldier on solo to 61. This season, for the first time, record-threatening sluggers came from separate teams. And though Mark McGwire and Sammy Sosa made it a point to emphasize that they were not competing against each other, they no doubt pushed and prodded each other into uncharted territory. While each man supplied singular great moments, the times that exemplified the specialness of their magical mystery tour were those they shared—such as their embrace after Mark first reached number 62, and, especially, their dual press conferences, at which Sammy usually stole the show with genuinely amusing one-liners (not easy to do in a second language).

Their joy and camaraderie were palpable. Neither would be "disappointed" if the other won the race for the record. McGwire, who set the unfathomable mark of 70 home runs, had said: "What Sammy and I have done, whoever is on top, nobody should be disappointed. How can you walk away disappointed? You can't. It's impossible." Sammy, who finished "second" with a mind-boggling 66, had said: "Disappointed for what? I didn't think for any moment I would get disappointed. I'm happy for Mark. I'm happy for myself. Mark is my friend." Sammy Sosa and Mark McGwire will likely be remembered as the friendliest and most gracious of competitors: two amazing ballplayers of different backgrounds and temperaments, who apportioned equal parts dignity, humility, and appreciation in their historic chase; two heroic sluggers whose signature home run salutes involved complicated hand signals and gesticulations, but who both touched one place: their hearts; two common men with uncommon skills who traveled great distances in order to come home; and, finally, two professionals who ultimately found the real pleasure was in the process, the doing, the being, the going ... going, gone. **Baseball** is a **game** of inches, measured in feet, played in yards, defined by **competition**, transcended by **camaraderie**. There's more to it, of course. **Much** more.

118

MARK McGWIRE 1998 HOME RUN LOG

HR	DATE	PITCHER	TEAM
69/70	Sept. 27	Thurman/Pavano	Expos
67/68	Sept. 26	Hermanson/Bullinger	Expos
66	Sept. 25	Bennett	Expos
65	Sept. 20	Karl	Brewers
64	Sept. 18	Roque	Brewers
63	Sept. 15	Christiansen	Pirates
62	Sept. 8	Trachsel	Cubs
61	Sept. 6	Morgan	Cubs
60	Sept. 4	Reyes	Reds
58/59	Sept. 2	Edmondson/ Stanifer	Marlins
56/57	Sept. 1	Hernandez/ Pall	Marlins
55	Aug. 30	Martinez	Braves
54	Aug. 26	Speier	Marlins
53	Aug. 23	Rincon	Pirates
52	Aug. 22	Cordova	Pirates
51	Aug. 20	Reed	Mets
50	Aug. 20	W Blair	Mets
49	Aug. 19	M Karchner	Cubs
48	Aug. 19	Mulholland	Cubs
47	Aug. 11	B Jones	Mets
46	Aug. 8	Clark	Cubs
45	July 28	Myers	Brewers
44	July 26	J Thomson	Rockies
43	July 20	Boehringer	Padres
41/42	July 17	Bohanon/Osuna	Dodgers
39/40	July 12	Bergman/Elarton	Astros
38	July 11	Wagner	Astros
37	June 30	Rusch	Royals
36	June 27	Trombley	Twins
35	June 25	Burba	Indians
34	June 24	Wright	Indians
33	June 18	Reynolds	Astros
32	June 17	Lima	Astros
31	June 12	Benes	Astros
30	June 10	Parque	White Sox
29	June 8	Bere	White Sox
28	June 5	Hershiser	Giants
27	May 30	Ashby	Padres
26	May 29	Miceli	Padres
25	May 25	J Thomson	Rockies
24	May 24	Nen	Giants
22/23	May 23	R Rodriguez/Johnstone	Giants
21	May 22	Gardner	Giants
18/19/20	May 19	Green (2)/Gomes	Phillies
17	May 18	J Sanchez	Marlins
16	May 16	L Hernandez	Marlins
15	May 14	Millwood	Braves
14	May 12	Wagner	Brewers
13	May 8	R Reed	Mets
12	May 1	Beck	Cubs
11	April 30	Pisciotta	Cubs
10	April 25	Spradlin	Phillies
9	April 21	T Moore	Expos
8	April 17	Whiteside	Phillies
5/6/7	April 14	Suppan (2)/ Manuel	Diamondbacks
4	April 4	Wengert	Padres
3	April 3	Langston	Padres
2	April 2	Lankford	Dodgers
1	March 31	R Martinez	Dodgers

SAMMY SOSA 1998 HOME RUN LOG

HR	DATE	PITCHER	TEAM
66	Sept. 25	Lima	Astros
64/65	Sept. 22	Roque/Henderson	Brewers
63	Sept. 16	Boehringer	Padres
61/62	Sept. 13	Patrick/Plunk	Brewers
60	Sept. 12	De Los Santos	Brewers
59	Sept. 11	Pulsipher	Brewers
58	Sept. 5	Lawrence	Pirates
57	Sept. 4	Schmidt	Pirates
56	Sept. 2	Bere	Reds
55	Aug. 31	Tomko	Reds
54	Aug. 30	Kile	Rockies
53	Aug. 28	Thomson	Rockies
52	Aug. 26	Tomko	Reds
50/51	Aug. 23	Lima(2)	Astros
49	Aug. 21	Hershiser	Giants
48	Aug. 19	Bottenfield	Cardinals
47	Aug. 16	Bergman	Astros
45/46	Aug. 10	Ortiz/Brock	Giants
44	Aug. 8	Croushore	Cardinals
43	Aug. 5	Benes	Diamondbacks
42	July 31	Wright	Rockies
41	July 28	Wolcott	Diamondbacks
39/40	July 27	Blair/Embree	Diamondbacks
38	July 26	R Reed	Mets
37	July 22	M Batista	Expos
36	July 17	Ojala	Marlins
35	July 10	Karl	Brewers
34	July 9	Juden	Brewers
33	June 30	Embree	Diamondbacks
32	June 25	Moehler	Tigers
31	June 24	Greisinger	Tigers
30	June 21	Ty Green	Phillies
28/29	June 20	Beech/Borland	Phillies
26/27	June 19	Loewer (2)	Phillies
25	June 17	Patrick	Brewers
22/23/24	June 15	Eldred (3)	Brewers
21	June 13	Portugal	Phillies
20	June 8	Hawkins	Twins
19	June 7	Baldwin	White Sox
18	June 6	C Castillo	White Sox
17	June 5	Parque	White Sox
16	June 3	L Hernandez	Marlins
14/15	June 1	Dempster/O Henriquez	Marlins
12/13	May 27	Winston/Gomes	Phillies
10/11	May 25	Millwood/Cather	Braves
9	May 22	G Maddux	Braves
8	May 16	Sullivan	Reds
7	May 3	Politte	Cardinals
6	April 27	J Hamilton	Padres
5	April 24	I Valdes	Dodgers
4	April 23	Miceli	Padres
3	April 15	Cook	Mets
2	April 11	Telford	Expos
1	April 4	M Valdes	Expos

About the Author

Lee R. Schreiber is an award-winning writer and editor who has contributed to *GQ, The New York Times Magazine, TV Guide,* and *Men's Life*, among many other publications. He is the author of eight books. As a second baseman, he displays rare flashes of power.

Acknowledgments

For Major League Baseball:
Donald S. Hintze, Director of Publishing
Faith Matorin, Art Director
Rich Pilling, Manager, Major League Baseball Photos
Paul Cunningham, Administrator, Major League Baseball Photos

For HarperEntertainment, a division of HarperCollins*Publishers*:
Robert Wilson, Senior Editor
Kristin Hillen, Editorial Assistant
Jeannette Jacobs, Art Director, Interior
John Silbersack, Senior Vice President and Publishing Director
Mauro DiPreta, Executive Editor
Mark Landau, Vice President of Special Sales
Amy Wasserman, Marketing Director
Gene Mydlowski, Art Director, Cover
Dianne Walber, Director of Production
Helen Moore, Publishing Manager
April Benavides, Production Editor
Joie Cooney, Business Manager

Photo Credits
©1998 Scott Cunningham/Major League Baseball Photos: 40 left, 48; ©1998 Louis DeLuca/MLB Photos: 7; ©1998 Tom DiPace/MLB Photos: 52; ©1998 Dan Donovan/MLB Photos: 2–3, 4, 12–13, 93 right; ©1998 David Durochik/MLB Photos: 15, 16 left; ©1998 Stephen Green/MLB Photos: 21; ©Major League Baseball Properties: i, vi, 8, 11, 32-33, 120; National Baseball Hall of Fame: 17, 31, 34, 94, 99, 100, 102, 104, 106, 108, 110, 112; ©1998 Joe Picciolo/MLB Photos: 63, 64-65, 69, 117; ©1998 Rich Pilling/MLB Photos: ii, iii, 9, 26 left, 27, 38-39, 40 right, 41 right, 45, 47, 51, 55, 56-57, 58, 59, 70, 71, 72-73, 78, 90, 96-97, 114-115; ©1998 John Reid III/MLB Photos: 41 left, 43; ©1998 Bob Rosato/MLB Photos: iv, v, 6, 10, 87, 88–89; ©1998 William R. Sallaz/MLB Photos: 14; ©1998 Rob Shanahan/MLB Photos: 26 right, 36; Milo Stewart, Jr./National Baseball Hall Of Fame Library: 22, 23, 93 left; ©1998 Bill Stover/MLB Photos: 5, 61, 68, 74, 76-77, 82, 83; ©1998 Ron Vesely/MLB Photos: 16 right, 19, 24, 28-29, 59 bottom, 66-67, 80-81, 84, 92 left, 92 right.